To:

_____

From:

_____

Date:

_____

# GodMoments *for* Women

## Carolyn Larsen

christian
art gifts®

*GodMoments for Women*

Copyright © 2012 Carolyn Larsen
All rights reserved.

Developed in co-operation with Educational Publishing Concepts

© 2012 Christian Art Gifts, RSA
        Christian Art Gifts Inc., IL, USA

Designed by Christian Art Gifts

Images used under license from Shutterstock.com

Scripture quotations are taken from the *Holy Bible,* New International
Version® NIV®. Copyright © 1973, 1978, 1984, 2011 by International
Bible Society. Used by permission of Zondervan Publishing House.
All rights reserved.

Printed in China

ISBN 978-1-77036-904-7

# Introduction

Hey there,

I can just hear what you are thinking ... "My life is CRAZY busy. I cannot ... simply cannot fit one more thing into my schedule. Sure, I want to spend time with God ... but WHEN?" Yes, I hear you and I'm right there with you.

We seem to live our lives on the proverbial hamster wheel and we make choices every day as to what we have time for and what we have to let go. But, the truth is that starting your day by spending a moment with God (if you only have a moment) will definitely improve your day.

So, take a few moments to focus your heart on the truth of His presence with you in every circumstance. Allow His love to guide you through this busy day in all you do and in all your relationships. A God Moment makes a God Day!

# Hanging On
# for Dear Life

The fear of the Lord leads to life;
then one rests content, untouched by trouble.
- Proverbs 19:23 -

**Life is so ... constant.** Perhaps that is because we women are, by nature, caretakers for many of those around us – family and friends. Consequently, we are seldom dealing with our own issues. We're adding in the cares, concerns and stresses of others to our own.

Whew – that much care can take us to the end of our rope very quickly. You know the end of the rope ... that's the point where the cares, concerns and stresses we are dealing with are so deep that we think we can't go on. We don't have hope that things will ever get better. So, what do we do when the end of the rope is slipping through our hands? How do we manage to tie a knot and hang on?

We remember ... remember that our strength comes from God. Remember that He loves us and our friends and family more than we can imagine. Remember that God can be trusted. We just need to hang on and He will take care of us.

When you get to the end of your rope,
tie a knot and hang on.
*Franklin D. Roosevelt*

# Friend Talk

"For where two or three gather in My Name, there am I with them."
- Matthew 18:20 -

Perhaps you've had the experience of reuniting with a long-lost friend. A person you were once very close to but haven't spent time with in a very long time. When you get back together you pick up conversation right where you left off. It's like you've never been apart and you keep talking until late into the night. Then, even after you've gone to bed, your brain keeps thinking about the conversation so sleep evades you.

Why is this worth thinking about? Because good communication with good friends is a gift from God. It means there are people in your life who care about you and with whom you share memories. It means that the conversation you have with them is important enough to keep you thinking about it for a long time. Thank God for good friends and ask for help to be a good friend to others yourself!

Good communication is as stimulating as black coffee, and just as hard to sleep after.
*Anne Morrow Lindbergh*

# You Matter to God

We are God's handiwork,
created in Christ Jesus to do good works,
which God prepared in advance for us to do.
- Ephesians 2:10 -

Are you discouraged about your lot in life? Do you find yourself getting crabby about the job you go to each day but do not enjoy at all? Are you having trouble getting along with your teenagers? Do you feel unappreciated and under-valued?

Well, there is one strong first step to changing each of these situations ... change your attitude.

You can't change other people's behavior so don't waste your time on that. The only thing you can change is your attitude toward what's happening. You can do that by remembering that God values you very much. He knows your situation and even in difficult times, He has a purpose for you and is aware of everything you're dealing with.

Find your value in Him. That will change your attitude which just might change your situation.

Human beings, by changing the inner
attitudes of their minds, can change
the outer aspects of their lives.

*William James*

# Holy Partnership

As the body without the spirit is dead,
so faith without deeds is dead.

- James 2:26 -

Faith in God is the fuel that gets you through the tough times in life, right? You trust Him. You believe His word. You know He loves you and has a plan for your life. But, many times ... most times ... when you pray for God's guidance or intervention, He doesn't expect you to settle down in your easy chair and eat bonbons while He does all the work.

You are God's partner in His work in the world. So, don't be surprised if your prayers are answered by the birth of an idea to do something yourself. What do you do then? First, be certain the idea is God-directed, test it through prayer and maybe bounce it off a trusted friend. When you know God has planted the thought ... get busy! And thank Him for trusting you to be His partner!

Faith can move mountains, but don't be
surprised if God hands you a shovel.

*Anonymous*

# True Beauty

Let the king be enthralled by your beauty;
honor Him, for He is Your Lord.
- Psalm 45:11 -

Let's be honest, women. Many of us spend a lot of time, energy and money trying to reach some level of the world's standard for beauty. The emphasis on looking younger, thinner, having the right style, clothes, make-up, hairstyle and whatever else consumes us.

Why? Seriously ... why? The truth is that kind of beauty *is* only skin-deep. True beauty comes from more than make-up or designer clothes. It comes from spending time in the presence of the Beautiful One – Jesus, and getting to know Him well enough that His beauty absorbs into you and you can reflect it to others. True, honest, lasting beauty comes only from being like Jesus.

I'm tired of all this nonsense about beauty being only skin-deep. That's deep enough. What do you want – an adorable pancreas?

*Jean Kerr*

# Personal Battles

But the fruit of the Spirit is love, joy,
peace, forbearance, kindness, goodness,
faithfulness, gentleness and self-control.
Against such things there is no law.
- Galatians 5:22-23 -

A store clerk is just downright rude. A waitress totally messes up your order. Another driver cuts you off in traffic. A usually cordial neighbor completely ignores you. What's your typical response to these kinds of experiences? Do you let yourself go to the dark side ... matching the rude and inconsiderate behavior of others?

Don't go there. Give people the benefit of the doubt and understand that every person who crosses your path is fighting some battle on some level. No one's life is without problems; at least not for very long. So, even as you are dealing with your own struggles and perhaps expecting others to just know that and treat you kindly; realize that each of them is also dealing with their own struggles ... so they each need YOU to treat them kindly.

Be kind, for everyone you meet
is fighting a hard battle.
*Plato*

# Rolling with Life

"I know the plans I have for you," declares the
Lord, "plans to prosper you and not to harm you,
plans to give you hope and a future."

- Jeremiah 29:11 -

One true constant in life is change. Don't
you love it when life settles into a pattern so you
can think, "OK, this is what my life is going to be
like." However, almost before that sentence is out,
something changes. Something big.

How many times have you seen your life or
someone else's change in just a split second? An
accident, a diagnosis or someone else's choice changes
everything. While changes can be disconcerting or
even upsetting, they do not have to mean the end of
relationships, careers, friendships or families. They
only mean that things have changed. You have to roll
with the punches ... adjust and accept.

How do you do that? Don't forget that God is
in the process. Remember that even in the midst of
changes that come so regularly, the only real constant
is that God does not change. He is in control. He
loves you. He has a plan. So, go with the flow and
hang on to God for the journey!

A bend in the road is not the end of the road ...
unless you fail to make the turn.

*Anonymous*

# The Best Is Yet to Come

Teach us to number our days,
that we may gain a heart of wisdom.

- Psalm 90:12 -

Growing older sometimes seems like a not so funny joke. One day you realize that when you tell your legs to run, they say, "Huh uh." Another day you look in the mirror and an unfamiliar face with wrinkles, age spots and gray hair looks back at you. Where did that come from?

Some women fight to stay young and sometimes that battle takes extreme measures. That's a matter of choice, of course. Other women age gracefully and elegantly. Of course, the truth is, everyone ages and there is nothing you can do to stop it, except die, of course. So, why not advance into aging? Accept it and appreciate the wisdom that aging brings. Appreciate that there are some things that the young have to deal with that are no longer issues for older people.

There are some good things about growing older. Focus on those.

Age is an issue of mind over matter.
If you don't mind, it doesn't matter.

*Mark Twain*

# Side by Side

Two are better than one, because they have a
good return for their labor: If either of them falls
down, one can help the other up. But pity anyone who falls and has no one to help them up.

*- Ecclesiastes 4:9-10 -*

Women are very aware of the importance of
relationships. Our friendships and family relationships
are so important to us. It's good to know that someone
is walking with you through life. In the happy times,
it is nice to have someone with whom to celebrate.
Shared joy has double the happiness.

In difficult times it is nice to have someone to
hold your hand and pray with you; even to cry with
you. Shared sorrow has less power. Thank God for
the people in your life who share your joys and your
sorrows. Then thank them for their care. Remember
that you can be the person who does that for others.
Open your heart wide enough to share someone else's
joy and sorry. Let them be sure of your presence.

Piglet sidled up to Pooh from behind.
"Pooh?" he whispered. "Yes, Piglet?"
"Nothing," said Piglet, taking Pooh's paw.
"I just wanted to be sure of you."

*A. A. Milne*

# Advice Givers versus Work Doers

Like apples of gold in settings
of silver is a ruling rightly given.
- Proverbs 25:11 -

You know her ... the woman who has advice
about literally everything. She always knows a better
way of doing things than you. She has advice for you
on marriage, parenting, jobs, ministry and even on
how to wear your hair. The thing is, the woman who
knows the best way to do things but never actually
does things herself probably doesn't know what she's
talking about.

It takes experience, which means trying, failing
and trying a different way, to know the better way
to do something. So, as old Mr. Franklin said, "Well
done is better than well said." Well done gives you
the right to be heard and the experience to speak
from. When you want advice, go to someone who has
walked with God for a while and who has actually
done the thing to need advice on. That will be the best
advice you can get.

Well done is better than well said.
*Benjamin Franklin*

# Actions Speak Louder than Words

Jesus replied: "'Love the Lord your God with all your heart and with all your soul and with all your mind.' This is the first and greatest commandment. And the second is like it: 'Love your neighbor as yourself.'"

*- Matthew 22:37-39 -*

We're told in the Bible that the greatest commandment is to love God above all else and to love our neighbor as we love ourselves. Sounds simple, right? It should be and it usually is, but sometimes it takes some thought.

Because other people cannot hear your thoughts or see what is inside your mind, they can't know what your intentions are. You have to put action to your intentions in such a way that others can see your love and care. It also is important to think about how your actions will be perceived. What says "I care" to one person may not say anything to another. So ... think about who you are reaching out to and try to understand what action would speak into her heart.

Let your heart of gold show to others by what you do.

Remember, people will judge you by your actions, not your intentions.
You may have a heart of gold –
but so does a hard-boiled egg.

*Anonymous*

# Getting Up
# One More Time

The eternal God is your refuge,
and underneath are the everlasting arms.
- Deuteronomy 33:27 -

Do you read the quote below and think, "How? How can I keep getting up when I'm tired and overwhelmed by life? Where can I find the strength to pull myself to standing after seven falls?" That's OK. You can feel that way because falling down (or being knocked down) over and over and over is tiring.

You may stand up the first few times even though you are battered, bruised and tired. But, close your eyes and imagine this scene: you have fallen one more time but the strength and will to get up is not in your heart. Then suddenly you feel two strong arms sliding beneath you and lifting you up. The Holy Spirit. God Himself will lift you when you haven't got the strength to get up. He will hold you tightly to Himself.

Draw closer to Him now and know that His strength will be there any time you turn to Him. He doesn't *have* to be your strength – He *wants* to be your strength.

Fall seven times, stand up eight.
Japanese Proverb

# Birthday Blessings

Being confident of this, that He who began
a good work in you will carry it on to
completion until the day of Christ Jesus.

- Philippians 1:6 -

When the first number in your age changes, does it cause you to stop and evaluate where you are in life? Do you look back to your youth and recall the plans you made, the dreams you had, the mountains you were going to climb, and think ... well that didn't happen? Does it sometimes feel as though the big things of life have passed you by and now you are done?

Do not be content, at any age, to settle down in a rocking chair and just wait for your ticket to heaven. There are no retirees from God's work. Sure, your work may change as you grow older. But, it is possible that as one thing in life wanes, another thing rises to the forefront and you may discover a whole new dream of how to serve God and serve others. Look around, pay attention, dream big. Life isn't over yet!

It is possible at any age to discover a lifelong
desire you never knew you had.

*Robert Brault*

# Strong Enough to Forgive

"Do not judge, and you will not be judged.
Do not condemn, and you will not be
condemned. Forgive, and you will be forgiven."
- Luke 6:37 -

How much energy do you spend holding on to anger? Now, don't get defensive. Just admit that it does take a lot of energy to stay mad at someone. Mental energy is expended and heart energy is drained. You may think you are strong because you are holding on to your anger and standing firm to make your point.

The truth is that it takes more strength to forgive someone and move on. Weak people can't forgive because they can't move on. Strong people can let go of hurt and anger and know that it will be OK – it doesn't mean that the other person "won". You are probably very thankful for forgiveness when you are the one being forgiven. And, undoubtedly, you are thankful that God Himself doesn't hold on to anger.

His forgiveness is total and final. If it wasn't, your life and future would look completely different, right? He is your model. Be strong and forgive. Move on with life.

The weak can never forgive.
Forgiveness is the attribute of the strong.
*Mahatma Gandhi*

# Plan Ahead!

Set your minds on things above,
not on earthly things. For you died,
and your life is now hidden with Christ in God.
- Colossians 3:2-3 -

If you were seriously ill, would you want to be treated by a doctor who had not gone to medical school? Probably not. You would prefer a doctor who had gone to medical school and graduated first in his class, right? You want him to be prepared for however he needs to treat you.

Do you expect anything less of yourself? Do you prepare for whatever may come up in your life? What does that mean? Well, the best way to prepare yourself for life is to start every day in God's Word. Spend time with Him. Then whatever life brings each day, you will be ready.

You shouldn't jump into a deep friendship and trust with God in the middle of a crisis if you haven't done your part to know Him before the crisis happens.

Dig the well before you are thirsty.
Chinese Proverb

# Work in Progress

"Whoever has will be given more, and they will have an abundance. Whoever does not have, even what they have will be taken from them."
- Matthew 25:29 -

So, you're growing older. Life has changed. You are retired ... even from the Sunday school class you used to teach.

Do you feel that your work is done and so is your usefulness? There's no doubt that things change as you grow older. Your body will no longer do the things it used to do – even the things your brain tells it to do. So, it's harder to do some things and it takes longer to do what you used to do. But, that doesn't mean that your usefulness to God is gone.

News Flash ... as long as He leaves you on this earth there will be ways you can serve Him. Granted, things may change and the opportunities you are given will change. But, as long as you have breath, you can serve God and love people. Get creative ... you might find something you love to do!

Here is the test to find whether your mission on earth is finished. If you're alive, it isn't.
*Richard Bach*

# Resolutions

"Come now, let us settle the matter," says
the Lord. "Though your sins are like scarlet,
they shall be as white as snow; though they
are red as crimson, they shall be like wool."
- Isaiah 1:18 -

Do you make New Year's resolutions? Do you
try very hard to keep your well-intentioned resolutions
but find by February 1 that you've slipped back into
your old ways? So, determined to persevere, you set
March 1 as the new resolution date! How long does
this go on? How hard are you on yourself that you
can't start life with a clean new page with each vowed
resolution? Well, stop it.

You can turn over new leaves day after day after day
but the sin in your heart will always be there ... until
you get to heaven. The gift is that the story of your life
can be written on pages that do have scratched-out
lines. God sees through the failures and weaknesses of
broken resolutions and because of Jesus' death on the
cross all He sees are sparkling white pages!

You will turn over many a futile new leaf till you
learn we must all write on scratched-out pages.
*Mignon McLaughlin*

# Common Sense

Trust in the Lord with all your heart and
lean not on your own understanding;
in all your ways submit to Him,
and He will make your paths straight.
- Proverbs 3:5-6 -

God has power over everything in the world –
nature and nations and people. No argument, right?
Of course you believe that you can trust Him to take
care of you with His amazing power and wisdom.
But, do you sometimes leap into commitments and
situations without seeking God's guidance and put
yourself in dangerous or unwise places?

God will never lead you into a situation where He
cannot take care of you. But, God gave you a brain
and a conscience, too. So use those tools as you make
choices about things you do. You can, of course, call
on God to protect you, guide you and shelter you. But
don't leap into situations where you put yourself in
harm's way and then cry out to God to save you. God
will take care of you, but stay close to Him and seek
His guidance and direction in your life ... before the
fact, not after.

God is good, but never dance in a small boat.
*Irish Saying*

# A Good Night's Sleep

Show me Your ways, Lord, teach me Your paths.
- Psalm 25:4 -

There is no way to measure the value of a good night's sleep, especially when life is stressful and you badly need rest. Of course, you would not deliberately do things that would cause sleepless nights. But think about this: impetuousness causes sleepless nights.

Making decisions that are not thought through and especially not prayed through will always ... ALWAYS ... cause sleepless nights. Before making decisions, take some time to "live" with the choice you have made. Give God a chance to change your mind or guide you in a different direction. If your decision keeps you awake at night, there is a good chance that God is speaking to you and trying to change your mind.

So, sleep on the decision, and spend time praying before you actually make the decision! Then ... sweet dreams!

It is better to sleep on things beforehand
than lie awake about them afterwards.
*Baltasar Gracian*

# No Whining Zone

Do everything without grumbling or arguing,
so that you may become blameless and pure,
"children of God without fault in a warped
and crooked generation." Then you will
shine among them like stars in the sky.
- Philippians 2:14-15 -

Complainers ... they suck the life right out of you, don't they? Do you avoid a friend who is constantly complaining about pretty much everything because you are pulled down by her complaining?

It's so easy to jump on the complaining train. However, people who complain about everything but make no investment to enforce change ... really lose the right to complain. How does a complaining spirit reflect your relationship with Jesus? Criticizing and complaining about others shows very little Christ-like love. It shows little teamwork to make the world, family, church (whatever you're complaining about) a better place or more effective for Christ.

God gave you a brain and energy and creativity. Use it. Don't complain ... get busy and make change happen. And, encourage any complaining friends to join you in making changes!

If you have time to whine and complain
about something then you have the
time to do something about it.
*Anthony J. D'Angelo*

# No Suffering

Even though I walk through the darkest valley,
I will fear no evil, for You are with me;
Your rod and Your staff, they comfort me.
- Psalm 23:4 -

Some experiences in life are painful. There's no getting away from that. Pain happens to everyone. No one escapes difficulties.

However, the way a woman approaches those difficulties is very telling of her attitude toward life and her opinion of God's sovereignty. The ability to accept pain as part of life but deny its control over her life shows an optimistic attitude and trust in God's plan, control and love. Some women settle into painful situations and allow themselves to wallow in the pain, leading to consuming suffering. Maybe that happens because they secretly enjoy the attention the suffering brings. Or maybe it's because they truly do not know how to rest in God.

Letting go of control and accepting pain as part of life but realizing that God knows about it and will walk through it with you ... that stops you from sinking into the pit of suffering. Try it.

Pain is inevitable. Suffering is optional.
M. Kathleen Casey

# Words in Action

All Scripture is God-breathed and is useful for teaching, rebuking, correcting and training in righteousness, so that the servant of God may be thoroughly equipped for every good work.

- 2 Timothy 3:16-17 -

No doubt you've met people who seem to have all the answers. This type of woman is well read, sure of her beliefs, convinced she is right and quite willing to try to sway you to agree with all she believes.

However, there is often an important element missing in the life of this strong-willed and opinionated person. That is ... action. Knowing the truth is not enough. Knowing Scripture is not enough. Quoting Scripture verse and reference and even intent is NOT enough. Action – living out the truths of Scripture day in and day out are more important than head knowledge.

Quoting Scriptures about love but treating others rudely and unkindly proves that the verses mean nothing to the one quoting them.

How will unbelievers know the truth of Scripture if it is only quoted but not lived?

Knowing is not enough; we must apply.
Willing is not enough; we must do.

*Johann Wolfgang von Goethe*

# Unnecessary Words

No human being can tame the tongue.
It is a restless evil, full of deadly poison.
- James 3:8 -

God tells us in the words of Scripture how very much damage the tongue can do. Think about it ... friendships can be destroyed by secrets revealed or thoughtless comments made. Reputations can be damaged by half-truths spoken or even truths spoken which do not need to be made public.

Regardless of what you know about another person, think about whether it is necessary for you to tell others what you know. Are you absolutely certain that the things you know are true? What good can come from speaking it? How will others be affected by the words you speak? How will other people's opinions of you be changed by knowing what you have said about another person?

Even more importantly, how will their opinions of the God you claim to follow be impacted? Remember that all you do and say reflects on Him.

Never tell evil of a man, if you do not know it for certainty, and if you know it for a certainty, then ask yourself, "Why should I tell it?"

Johann K. Lavater

# Real Friendship

Greater love has no one than this:
to lay down one's life for one's friends.
- John 15:13 -

Real friends are more valuable than precious jewels. Friends who know your rough edges – your struggles, fears, weaknesses and like you anyway are absolutely priceless.

But, if you are able to be yourself, and you have a friend who sees you and likes you anyway, thank the Lord. Of course, this works in reverse, too. Are you the kind of friend who sees the realness of your friends and likes them anyway? If you're going to be nit-picky about another person's foibles, weaknesses and character flaws, you probably will not have many true friends.

Be thankful for your friends who love you no matter what. Make every effort to be the kind of friend to others as you show the kind of forgiving love and grace that is shown to you every day by your heavenly Father!

Your friend is the man who knows
all about you, and still likes you.
Elbert Hubbard

# No Complaining Zone

It is good to praise the Lord and make music to
Your name, O Most High, proclaiming Your love
in the morning and Your faithfulness at night.
- Psalm 92:1-2 -

Here's a challenge for you ... for three days
write down everything you find yourself complaining
about. Every situation. Every annoyance. Everything
that makes you angry. At the end of the three days,
look over the list you've made. Then, compare it with
stories in the news of what people around the world
are dealing with.

The news may tell you of hurricanes, tsunamis,
earthquakes, fires, or daily problems of people who
do not have clean water available to drink or who can
find no food. As you compare the two lists, does yours
kind of drop in importance? You may realize that while
your problems are annoying or inconvenient, they are
not severe enough to be considered life threatening.

Perhaps this exercise will help you to complain less
and pray more for those around the world who face
real problems.

If you break your neck, if you have nothing to eat,
if your house is on fire, then you have a problem.
Everything else is inconvenience.

*Robert Fulghum*

# Choose Wisely

This is the confidence we have in
approaching God: that if we ask
anything according to His will, He hears us.
- 1 John 5:14 -

Are you a decisive woman? Or are you a people pleaser who has difficulty making decisions because you don't want to hurt anyone or cause anyone problems? Do you put off making decisions or choices as long as possible ... until sometimes it is too late to make the choice?

You may think you've avoided the difficulty, but in reality you've just compounded your problem because not to decide is, actually, to decide. When a decision needs to be made or a choice is before you, something will eventually happen. If you do not make your choice then you've lost the power to be involved in the situation or its outcome.

So, when a choice is before you, take it to the Lord. Pray about it, seek His guidance, ask trusted Christian friends, then be brave and make your decision! Don't worry about offending or hurting others. God can take care of that, too!

When you have to make a choice and
don't make it, that is in itself a choice.
*William James*

# The Right Prayer

He said to them, "When you pray, say: 'Father,
hallowed be Your name, Your kingdom come.
Give us each day our daily bread.'"
- Luke 11:2-3 -

This is the prayer I should be praying:

"Dear God, forgive me for the many, many selfish prayers I've prayed. Prayers requesting (or demanding) more than I needed, ungrateful for all that I have.

Forgive me for thinking I deserve more than I have. Forgive me for not seeing that some people around the world do not even have the basic necessities such as clean drinking water. Forgive me for not being satisfied with my "daily bread" which meets my needs to get through each day, even if it doesn't give me what I want. Help me see the difference between need and want. And to be thankful for the needs You meet and then to pray diligently and passionately for others to have their needs met before I even whisper a prayer about my wants."

Yes, this is what I should be praying ... no, wait, this is what I WILL pray.

"Give us this day our daily bread" is probably
the most perfectly constructed and useful
sentence ever set down in the English language.

P. J. Wingate

# True Friendship

A friend loves at all times,
and a brother is born for a time of adversity.

- Proverbs 17:17 -

True friendship is an amazing gift. Some "friends" are glad to hang out with you when things are going well and you don't demand or need much support from them. Theirs is a "low investment" kind of friendship. They may be lots of fun to be with but when your life gets a bit complicated, they are history.

Real friends are certainly around when life is good. They enjoy partying with you, celebrating, laughing, talking and going out for fun lunches. The difference is that when you get a scary health diagnosis, you lose your job, a relationship breaks up, or a loved one passes ... the true friend comes closer, not farther away. A true friend shares your pain and stays close by to help you through it. If you have a friend like this, thank God for her and then thank her for her friendship!

A friend is the one who comes in when
the whole world has gone out.

*Grace Pulpit*

# Letting Go

"Ask and it will be given to you; seek and you will find; knock and the door will be opened to you. For everyone who asks receives; the one who seeks finds; and to the one who knocks, the door will be opened."

- Matthew 7:7-8 -

Are you a control freak? Do you knowingly attempt to micro-manage friends, co-workers, family members or situations? Does it make you feel weak when you are not in control? Does it sometimes feel as though you are caving in if you don't push to have your own way? Does it make you feel weak ... as though you have lost control?

Actually, the exact opposite is true. Being able to give up control takes incredible strength and having the strength to let go and let others make their own decisions is a sign of maturity.

It's hard to stand by and watch while a loved one or a friend makes choices that will cause them pain. You may want to leap in and fix things but must realize that others learn important lessons by making their own mistakes. So ... pray for your loved ones as they make decisions, but let them make their own choices.

Giving up doesn't always mean you are weak.
Sometimes it means that you
are strong enough to let go.

Anonymous

# Giving Space

If any of you lacks wisdom, you should ask God,
who gives generously to all without finding fault,
and it will be given to you.

- James 1:5 -

The quote below may seem kind of weird. But, if you live in a family, work around other people, have close friends ... you know that it's so true. Of course you want people you care about and spend time with to be happy. You certainly don't want to do anything to bring them unhappiness, right? You would never do that on purpose.

Well, let's be honest, there are times when you can bring happiness to others by spending time with them, giving advice and helping them. But, there are also times when the best thing you can do for them is to give them some space. Pray for the wisdom to know the difference between these two times ... then be strong enough and loving enough to follow the wisdom God gives you.

Never miss an opportunity to make others happy,
even if you have to leave them
alone in order to do it.

*Anonymous*

# Free Advice

The mouths of the righteous utter wisdom,
and their tongues speak what is just.
- Psalm 37:30 -

Some people love to give advice – you know who you are. Perhaps you have been the recipient of free advice on something as basic as how to discipline your children ... from a person who has no children. Or perhaps a friend constantly tells you how to handle issues in your career ... when she doesn't have a job.

Getting advice from people who have some kind of experience in similar situations is a wise thing to do. You can learn a lot from people who have been through similar experiences. But, when people freely offer advice and have absolutely no idea what you're going through, their advice may not be the best.

Be wise in the advice you listen to – even if it's from a good friend. Sift through all advice and pray for wisdom to listen to the right voices.

Never take the advice of someone who
has not had your kind of trouble.
Sidney J. Harris

# Song of Praise

The Lord is my strength and my shield;
my heart trusts in Him, and He helps me.
My heart leaps for joy,
and with my song I praise Him.

- Psalm 28:7 -

Real praise flows from the heart. It is an involuntary action that springs from the recognition of who God is and all that He does for you and in your life. It doesn't mean that you have full understanding of all He does.

Praise can even happen in the dark times when you can't seem to really connect with God. Because in those times, as in good times, something as beautiful as a sunset, as gentle as a butterfly, or as personal as a hug can remind you of God's pure love for you. Praise then flows from you in thankfulness for the reminder of God's presence and care for you. As a bird has a song to share, your song is praise to God and you can't help but sing.

A bird does not sing because it has an answer,
it sings because it has a song.

Chinese Proverb

# Learning from Loss

My soul yearns for You in the night;
in the morning my spirit longs for You.
When Your judgments come upon the earth,
the people of the world learn righteousness.

- Isaiah 26:9 -

OK ladies, what kind of loser are you? Don't be embarrassed by answering that question. Everyone loses once in a while, whether it's an athletic event, a boyfriend, a job, a friend or a contest of some kind.

If you haven't ever experienced losing, you've missed an important growth process in life. Losing is never easy; in fact it often hurts a lot, but your reaction to losing is very important. Getting angry and vowing to get even is not a good reaction. Giving up and never trying again is not a good reaction. A good reaction is to learn from the loss. Remember that most lessons in life are learned through difficulty. So, honestly ask yourself what you could have done better or how you could have tried harder.

Do not beat yourself up and get obsessive about it, but learn and grow. Next time you may win!

When you lose, don't lose the lesson.

*Anonymous*

# Exercise Queen

"Whoever serves Me must follow Me;
and where I am, My servant also will be.
My Father will honor the one who serves Me."
- John 12:26 -

Are you obsessive about exercising? How many hours do you work out? How many days a week? How about thinness? Are you obsessive about what you will and will not eat?

The media has created an unrealistic image of what the perfect female body should look like. Some women buy into that image and obsessively work themselves crazy trying to look like the models in magazines ... and for what? Are they happy as they spend all that time dieting and exercising? Do they ever feel they are truly thin enough? Now understand that this obsession goes beyond trying to live a healthy lifestyle, in fact it goes all the way to being unhealthy. Exercising and eating healthy are fine, but it is also important to accept the way God made you and appreciate your uniqueness.

Take care of yourself, but focus your real energy on being a woman who loves and serves God.

I've exercised with women so thin that
buzzards followed them to their cars.

*Erma Bombeck*

# Remember Ginger!

What is more, I consider everything
a loss because of the surpassing
worth of knowing Christ Jesus my Lord,
for whose sake I have lost all things.
I consider them garbage, that I may gain Christ.
- Philippians 3:8 -

OK, you do know who Fred and Ginger were, right? They made several movies together, all involving amazing dance routines. Fred Astaire was famous for his dance skills and Ginger Rogers was his favorite partner. Why is this of interest? Because some times and in some situations, women have to work twice as hard as men to get the same recognition and respect. Because of that effort some women struggle to understand their importance and worth.

The Fred and Ginger story simply points out that while the very talented man in this scenario gets most of the recognition ... the woman performed every skill that he did under much more difficult conditions. If you ever struggle with feelings of inadequacy, remember Ginger and celebrate every skill, talent and ability that God has given you!

Ginger Rogers did everything Fred Astaire did.
But she did it backwards and in high heels.

Anonymous

# Choosing Peace

Turn from evil and do good;
seek peace and pursue it.
- Psalm 34:14 -

It's a good day – you're meeting your BFF in your favorite restaurant for lunch. This is much needed time away from your husband, kids, work ... just good old girl talk.

However, you get settled at your table and wait and wait and wait. When the waitress finally makes her way to your table you discover that she has a serious attitude ... a bad attitude! What's your reaction to her attitude? You could insist on talking to the manager and report her poor service. Or, you could ignore her but make jokes about her behind her back. You and your friend could spend your entire meal ripping up the unfriendly waitress. Or ... you could try smiling at your waitress. Seriously, smile at her because you have no idea what put her in her foul mood and a friendly smile might be just what she needs to help turn her day around.

Instead of picking a fight, lay the groundwork for peace.

Peace begins with a smile.
Mother Teresa

# Side-by-Side Comparison

For by the grace given me I say to every one
of you: Do not think of yourself more highly
than you ought, but rather think of yourself
with sober judgment, in accordance with
the faith God has distributed to each of you.

- Romans 12:3 -

Now, don't get upset about this statement – it is absolutely meant to be humorous. But, there is a serious side, too. Many women compare themselves to other women. They notice other women's weight, clothing style, hairstyle, and any other thing that can possibly be a point of comparison. As they look at these things in other women, they measure how they fare next to these women. It becomes a silent and one-sided competition.

Finding one area where they "win" is cause for a private celebration. But what's the point of these comparisons? Life should not be all about a competition, but should be about being able to be yourself – the person God made you to be. So, try not to compete, but to befriend others and enjoy the differences between you and your friends.

The chief excitement in a woman's life
is spotting women who are fatter than she is.

Helen Rowland

# Slow Motion

Not that I have already obtained all this,
or have already arrived at my goal,
but I press on to take hold of that for
which Christ Jesus took hold of me.
- Philippians 3:12 -

Some things take soooooo long. Let's restate that – good things seem to take a long time – like losing weight. It takes so long and so much effort and discipline to lose weight, but only about 5 minutes to gain 10 pounds. Sigh.

Or establishing a good habit – it takes months of repetitiveness before an activity or action becomes a daily habit that you do without consciously thinking about it, but bad habits take root overnight, right? Positive changes in life, everything from losing weight to having a daily (that's EVERY DAY) quiet time seem to take a long time to lock in to your mind. It can get discouraging. But the message is – don't be so hard on yourself. Moving forward slowly is better than standing still because that would mean that no improvements are happening.

It takes steadiness and persistence to move slowly, but the end result is definitely worth it! Even moving slowly means you're moving somewhere.

Do not fear going forward slowly.
Fear only to stand still.
Chinese Proverb

# Used Up

I eagerly expect and hope that I will in no way be
ashamed, but will have sufficient courage so that
now as always Christ will be exalted in my body,
whether by life or by death. For to me,
to live is Christ and to die is gain.
- Philippians 1:20-21 -

Women are master multi-taskers. We are
known for the ability to keep several balls in the air at
one time and never let even one hit the ground. This
skill is a gift from God and often is what keeps multi-
member families functioning.

There is sometimes a tension that must be balanced
when a woman has a passion for some work or ministry
that takes her away from home. But, the balance can
be found, especially with an understanding family.
Wouldn't it be wonderful when the time comes to
stand before God to know that you've used every gift
and talent He entrusted to you? Even as you cared
for family and friends, you were intentionally and
purposefully partnered with Him in His work on this
earth.

What a privilege. What a joy.

When I stand before God at the end of my life,
I would hope that I would not have a
single bit of talent left, and could say,
"I used everything You gave me."

*Erma Bombeck*

# Age Appropriate Injuries

Be kind and compassionate to one another,
forgiving each other, just as in
Christ God forgave you.

- Ephesians 4:32 -

Unfortunately, most of the time wisdom is something that you only gain as you grow older. Think about this, when you were a young girl, what was the one thing that you wanted so badly? To grow up, right? You wanted the freedom and privileges that you saw older girls and women enjoying.

One thing that eager-to-grow-up-young-girls don't think about is that bigger girls have bigger problems. Since you've grown up have there been times when you've longed for the simplicity of childhood problems? Yes, they seemed so serious then, but now ... not so much. This is a good reminder though, that younger girls in your world, or even young women, have problems that to them are major crises.

Even though you know that in the big picture of life, their problems are not so serious, you should still be compassionate and empathetic toward them. Skinned knees or broken hearts – both hurt at the time.

Sometimes I wish I were a little kid again, skinned knees are easier to fix than broken hearts.

*Anonymous*

# Dream Big

Now listen, you who say, "Today or tomorrow
we will go to this or that city, spend a year there,
do business and make money."
Why, you do not even know what will happen
tomorrow. What is your life? You are a mist
that appears for a little while and then vanishes.
Instead, you ought to say, "If it is the Lord's will,
we will live and do this or that."

- James 4:13-15 -

You've met people like this – people who are told, "That won't work." Or, "That cannot be done." Their response is to get busy and do that impossible thing. It's exciting to be around people like that. The creativity seems to flow from them and encompass all who are around them. Energy, joy, positivity and success come with that kind of drive, too.

Have you ever had a yearning to try something but someone in your world poured cold water on your dream? Don't let them. Maybe God gave you that yearning for a reason. If He plants a dream in your heart then He will help you accomplish it – even if there are problems along the way.

Ask God to help you have the courage to try ... you never know what will happen!

You see things; and you say, "Why?" But I dream things that never were; and I say, "Why not?"

George Bernard Shaw

# No-Hate Zone

Whoever claims to love God yet hates a brother or sister is a liar. For whoever does not love their brother and sister, whom they have seen, cannot love God, whom they have not seen.

- 1 John 4:20 -

There is an old saying that there is a thin line between love and hate. Both are very intense emotions, but they are at opposite ends of the emotional spectrum.

Love comes so naturally and it flows from the heart. Hate (or at least extremely strong dislike) may start as a flash emotion but then it must be fed so it can grow and grow. That "feeding" takes time, energy and thought and it steals from the rest of your life.

Is it really worth it? Stealing the energy to hate someone means another part of your life is being cheated. So, what's a better idea? When you feel such anger toward another person, rather than letting it grow to anger, stop and pray for that person. It's difficult to pray for someone and hate them at the same time.

Hating people is like burning down your own house to get rid of a rat.

Harry Emerson Fosdick

# Cleansing Tears

He heals the brokenhearted
and binds up their wounds.
- Psalm 147:3 -

You've been out working in the garden all day. You're dirty and covered with perspiration. What do you do? Hop in the shower, of course. You wash and scrub and let the water and soap do their job so you come out squeaky clean. It feels good to be clean.

Did you know that tears can do the same kind of job for your emotions and your soul? The difficulties of life pile up – even small ones pile one on top of the other until you are weighed down by them. While crying cannot fix your problems or solve your crises, tears do give vent to the emotions – like letting steam out of a boiling pot. Tears relieve some of the pressure and then you can think a bit more clearly. So, in a way, tears do the same job as soap does for your body.

Tears clear away the stresses that make your viewpoint and thinking process cloudy. Some women feel that tears make them appear weak. That's too bad, because they do a wonderful job of relieving pressure. That's a good thing.

What soap is for the body, tears are for the soul.
*Jewish Proverb*

# God in Nature

In the beginning God created
the heavens and the earth.
- Genesis 1:1 -

Where is your "spot?" Where is that place where you go and no matter how chaotic and crazy your life has been, that place will bring you peace and help you center?

Some people find that peaceful closeness to God in the mountains. The awesome grandeur of majestic mountains shows God's power and creativity and remind us that the problems of earth can certainly be handled by God. Some find a sense of peace and perspective when they are near the ocean. Again, the massive body of water and the consistency of the tide and waves bring peace and comfort. Others enjoy a meadow setting; still others love the varied creativity of the woods.

Regardless of where the spot is where you feel calmed and closer to God, it is a place where you can appreciate God's creation ... His creativity, His power, His strength and His love. Being in this spot in creation gives you a God moment.

Nature is the art of God.
Ralph Waldo Emerson

# Roses Among the Thorns

God is our refuge and strength,
an ever-present help in trouble.
- Psalm 46:1 -

Did you ever snip roses from a bush; beautiful, red roses with their gentle, romantic scent? But as you reached in to grab the stem, a sharp thorn pricked your finger. That is so painful and your immediate thought might be – why do roses have to have thorns?

Well, there are reasons, such as the thorns protect the roses from being eaten by some animals, so the best-smelling roses may have the most thorns.

There is also the philosophical reason that roses remind us of love but loving relationships involve some prickly issues from time to time. The good reminder of roses and thorns is to focus on the roses ... the love in your life, not the thorns ... the problems in your life. Thank God for the good things and learn from the problems.

Instead of complaining that the rosebush is full of thorns, be happy that the thorn bush has roses.

*German Proverb*

# Keep On Keeping On

Consider it pure joy, my brothers and sisters,
whenever you face trials of many kinds,
because you know that the testing of your
faith produces perseverance. Let perseverance
finish its work so that you may be mature
and complete, not lacking anything.

- James 1:2-4 -

You have a dream – a dream God gave you. Perhaps it is to help a group of people who have serious needs. Perhaps it is to establish a ministry of some kind. Maybe you're trying to develop a new friendship. Of course you know that whatever it is will take time to become established. But, how much patience and persistence do you have? Can you stick it out through the roadblocks and problems that arise? Can you keep your focus on the goal you believe God has given you?

Sometimes people give up their dreams when the going gets rough ... just before the success arrives. Keep pressing on with whatever God has given you to do. Depend on God's planning to be your guide and His strength to move you forward, and you have a better chance of sticking with the dream God gave you. You can enjoy your partnership with God in accomplishing His work. Keep on keeping on!

Many of life's failures are people
who did not realize how close they
were to success when they gave up.

*Thomas Edison*

# Be Yourself

For You created my inmost being;
You knit me together in my mother's womb.
I praise You because I am fearfully
and wonderfully made;
Your works are wonderful,
I know that full well.
- Psalm 139:13-14 -

Do not live in mediocrity; to do so is an insult to your Creator. Do not compare yourself to others and long for the gift of music that one friend has or the blessing of riches that another enjoys. Be careful not to minimize what you have because the simplest of abilities, talents and interests that are given from God and then offered back to Him can bless others in ways you could possibly never imagine.

Be yourself. Use the talents you have, work in the passion of what God has given you. Do not think you are insignificant or that what you can do for others is of no importance – you don't know what they need. Find great joy in serving God and loving others in the ways you are most comfortable and which bring you happiness.

Give what you have. To someone,
it may be better than you dare to think.
Henry Wadsworth Longfellow

# God's Music

Let them praise the name of the Lord,
for at His command they were created,
and He established them for ever and ever –
He issued a decree that will never pass away.
- Psalm 148:5-6 -

Do you hear the music of the world around you or does the cacophony of life drown out the music? There is no doubt that the "sounds" of life get pretty loud sometimes. Sounds that come from relationships, family, work; even church commitments can be so overwhelming that you can't hear or feel the precious song of praise for who God is and what He does for you every day.

Can you find the time to hear the music that leads your heart to praise and worship God? Nature itself sings music that can bless your heart and remind you of God's love and care for you. Find a God moment in the beauty of His creation. Get away from the busyness and noise of life once in a while and listen for the whispers of God's voice in nature that can reconnect you to Him.

There's music in the sighing of a reed;
there's music in the gushing of a rill;
there's music in all things, if men had ears:
their earth is but an echo of the spheres.

*Lord Byron*

# Living in Love

Now about your love for one another we do not need to write to you, for you yourselves have been taught by God to love each other.

- 1 Thessalonians 4:9 -

No one enjoys being hurt. In fact, once a woman gets hurt, she may put a protective wall around her heart to keep that pain from ever invading her world again. Sometimes the hurt is a romantic hurt – a broken heart that she thinks will never heal. But sometimes the pain is betrayal at the hands of a friend. That's a difficult hurt to overcome. If you can't trust your friends ...

However, the protective covering that a woman puts over her heart to protect from the hurt, also prevents the blessing of joy that comes from true friendship and love. God did not create people to be isolated and alone. He planned for people to live in community and in relationships. God is love and His love is to flow through people, one to another. That can't happen if a person is cut off from caring and loving.

The walls we build around us to keep sadness out also keeps out the joy.

*Jim Rohn*

# Personal Decisions

"For God so loved the world that He gave His one and only Son, that whoever believes in Him shall not perish but have eternal life."
- John 3:16 -

Mom and Dad were active in their church. It seemed to you, as a young person, that every single time the church doors opened, your family was there. Every family meal began with prayers of thanks and family devotions were a staple for you. Mom and Dad's house rules for their kids were Scripture based and conservative. The bottom line is that there was never any doubt that your family was Christian.

Now, as you've grown up, have you carried on some of those traditions that you grew up with? There's nothing wrong with that – except that just because your mom and dad were Christian and raised you that way, doesn't mean you are Christian, too. The only way to salvation is to make a personal confession of faith.

You can't ride to heaven on someone else's coattails. So ... have you done it? Have you asked Jesus to be your Savior?

You've got to do your own growing,
no matter how tall your grandfather was.
*Irish Proverb*

# To Guilt or Not to Guilt

Let us draw near to God with a sincere heart
and with the full assurance that faith brings,
having our hearts sprinkled to cleanse
us from a guilty conscience and having
our bodies washed with pure water.

- Hebrews 10:22 -

There is a sneaky little tool that some women use very masterfully to get others to do what they want. That tool is GUILT. Yes, some of us are pros at making just the right comment that will stab a knife of guilt into the heart of a friend, family member or co-worker.

Guilt is powerful because it lays in the mind and heart and is not easy to ignore. It also has a repeating value because just a word here or there can reactivate the guilt. Of course, there are major negatives that go with this tool. Guilt destroys relationships. Guilt can actually make people sick. And, the biggest negative of all – guilt is not God's way of doing things.

His word suggests more honest and open communication between people – communication that speaks love, forgiveness and care between people.

Guilt ... the gift that keeps on giving.
*Erma Bombeck*

# Special Friendship

"A new command I give you:
Love one another. As I have loved you,
so you must love one another."
- John 13:34 -

Think about these scenarios: It is the middle of the night, you can't sleep because the big decision you must make won't let your mind rest.

You just got the best news of your life and you want to tell someone.

You have choices to make – new job, serious boyfriend, move to a new city, and you need to talk them through with someone.

You've had an argument with your boyfriend or husband and you just need to talk.

In each case, with whom do you want to talk? If you have a really close friend – a soul sister – it's probably her. Two really good friends can finish each other's sentences. They know what the other one is thinking. They have similar values and morals.

A good friend is a gift from God who can encourage you, challenge you and hold you accountable. Such a friend helps you become a better you.

What is a friend?
It is a single soul in two bodies.
*Aristotle*

# Keep Growing

You are my strength, I watch for You;
You, God, are my fortress,
my God on whom I can rely.
- Psalm 59:9-10 -

Change ... is seldom easy ... is seldom welcomed ... is absolutely necessary!

Think back over your life and the changes you have experienced. Did they, for the most part, result in good growth for you; even if it took some time for you to realize it? If there is no change in your life, you can easily settle into a rut of always doing things the same way for the same reason. Ruts grow deeper and deeper and become more and more difficult to get out of. You don't really want to stick in a rut until you're settled in your grave, right?

Ask God to help you embrace change as He moves you around and grows you into the person He wants you to be. No matter what your age, embrace change.

The only difference between a rut
and a grave are the dimensions.
*Ellen Glasgow*

# Looking for the Good

In Him our hearts rejoice,
for we trust in His holy name.
- Psalm 33:21 -

God's plan will not lead you where God's power cannot keep you. Of course, life has its bumps and bruises. There are good times and difficult times and the challenge is to find your God moment in both types of experience.

When do you praise and worship God? When it seems that life is going well and He is answering your prayers and you have relatively few problems? Sure, it is easy to praise then. But, when the bumps come along and you seem to be directed into u-turns, how do you adapt? When God is in control, there is no reason to expect the worst of a changing situation. In fact, you can look for the surprises of His new plan and see what He has new for you. Sort of like "when life hands you lemons, make lemonade". When you find yourself in the problems of life (the mud puddle) look for the blessing He will give (fish in your pockets)!

You can avoid having ulcers by adapting
to the situation: If you fall in the
mud puddle, check your pockets for fish.

*Anonymous*

# Worrier or Truster?

You will keep in perfect peace those whose
minds are steadfast, because they trust in You.

*- Isaiah 26:3 -*

OK, woman of faith ... what's your stance on worry? The Sunday school answer, of course, is that worry isn't necessary because you only need to trust God. Trusting God is a great privilege and comfort for a believer. But, how many women say the "I trust God" words while staying up at night worrying about things? How do you make the transition from all-night-worrier to full-out-truster?

Take it a step at a time. The next time you have an issue that causes you worry, give it to God. Just give it to Him – tell Him that you are going to give this issue to Him. Then, every time the urge pops up to take it back from Him and worry about it, intentionally and even aloud, state that this particular issue is God's to deal with.

Learning to trust God is a journey ... take the first step!

Every evening I turn my worries over to God.
He's going to be up all night anyway.

*Mary C. Crowley*

# Other Vision

Whatever you do, work at it with all your heart,
as working for the Lord, not for human masters.
- Colossians 3:23 -

Me. Myself. I. For too much of the population of middle-income (and up) people of the world, the majority of their time and focus is on themselves – protecting themselves, providing for themselves, figuring out how to get ahead. Oh, there might be the occasional short-term concern that comes after a huge natural disaster. It is true concern, but it doesn't last long enough.

Some people will travel to the site to work on the recovery after a tornado or tsunami. Some will send money to help people who are suffering. Sending money is good – it's important. Praying is also important. But there is a real blessing of taking time out of your schedule and leaving your own comfortable life to actually go work to help those who are suffering. It's a privilege. It's a blessing. It's the love of God with work clothes and gloves on.

You must give some time to your fellow men.
Even if it's a little thing, do something
for others – something for which you
get no pay but the privilege of doing it.
Albert Schweitzer

# Three-legged Races

I long to see you so that I may impart to you some spiritual gift to make you strong – that is, that you and I may be mutually encouraged by each other's faith.

- Romans 1:11-12 -

Three-legged races recall picnics of childhood that are sprinkled with competitions like foot races, watermelon seed spitting contests and gunny sack races. Great fun.

There is a pretty cool life lesson in the three-legged race, though. In that race, two competitors stand side by side and a leg from each competitor is tied together. That means that between them they have three legs. They then run a foot race. When one of the racers falls down, the partner helps her up. It's a fun race.

The lesson is that it's good to have friends and partners to help you when you fall down. They pick you up and encourage you to go on. So, stop right now and thank God for the good friends you have who help you up when you're down and who cheer you on in whatever you are doing.

Remember, we all stumble, every one of us.
That's why it's a comfort to go hand in hand.
*Emily Kimbrough*

# Who's in Charge?

So then, just as you received Christ Jesus
as Lord, continue to live your lives in Him,
rooted and built up in Him, strengthened
in the faith as you were taught,
and overflowing with thankfulness.

- Colossians 2:6-7 -

Dear God,

OK, I resign. I've been trying to run the universe ...
at least my part of it ... and I can't do it. I quit. I think
You'd better take the job back. You might not do
things the way I would or even the way I want You to,
but You do a pretty good job. I'm looking forward to
being able to sleep at night, knowing that You are in
charge and that You're taking care of things. Oh, I'm
sure there will be days when I try to grab back control,
but I will eventually catch myself and resign again.
Your track record is ... well, perfect. You don't always
work on my time frame, but Your schedule ends up
being perfect, so, again – I resign. Take over. Thanks.

Amen.

For peace of mind, resign as general
manager of the universe.

*Anonymous*

# The Worst Disease

Just as each of us has one body with many members, and these members do not all have the same function, so in Christ we, though many, form one body, and each member belongs to all the others.

- Romans 12:4-5 -

Mother Teresa knew about disease. She worked with the sickest of poor people. She saw horrific diseases that people had to live with. But, in her wisdom and sensitivity, Mother Teresa knew that there is something worse than physical illness.

Do you know anyone who feels unwanted? Someone who has few, if any, friends to care about her, share her joys and laughter or hold her and cry with her? A person who feels unwanted has no purpose in her day – no reason to get up in the morning and she doesn't feel that she has anything to contribute to the world. She may just feel invisible.

Look around you – do you see anyone who may feel this way? If so, you can be God's hands, voice and heart to her by befriending her and giving her a chance to matter to someone. Reach out – make a difference to someone!

The biggest disease today is not leprosy or tuberculosis, but rather the feeling of being unwanted.

*Mother Teresa*

# Prayer Appointment

"If My people, who are called by My name,
will humble themselves and pray and
seek My face and turn from their wicked ways,
then I will hear from heaven, and I will
forgive their sin and will heal their land."

- 2 Chronicles 7:14 -

If you're not serious about prayer – get serious.
You may intend to have a regular, disciplined prayer
life; you really do. But, it's hard. The busyness of life
and well, Satan himself, fights against that discipline.

You may find yourself praying when you feel like
it, which will probably be when there is some crisis in
your life and there is something you need God to do
for you. But, if you believe that prayer is conversation
with God, like conversation with a friend, why
wouldn't you pray on a regular basis? Prayer is an
opportunity to bring to God the things that concern
you and where you need His guidance and help. Set a
regular time each day to pray – to connect with God.
Try your best to keep that appointment, even if it's
only a few minutes. Staying connected to God and
bringing Him into the situations that concern you
gives you great power – His power!

Don't pray when you feel like it.
Make an appointment with the King and keep it.

*Corrie ten Boom*

# Light Your World

This is the message we have heard from
Him and declare to you: God is light;
in Him there is no darkness at all.
- 1 John 1:5 -

Darkness that is so black you can't even see your own hand in front of your face is terrifying. Darkness hides things. You can't see what you're facing. You can't see what is around you. Just a tiny beam of light makes a difference in the darkness.

Think about the darkness that people who do not know Jesus live in. The light of the world is Jesus but they do not know Him. As a child of God you have the privilege of bringing light into the world around you. One source of the light is the love in your own heart. The Holy Spirit in your heart is the true source of all light and sometimes you reflect His light into the world around you.

By being the light or the reflector of light, you have the opportunity to bring God moments into the lives of others!

There are two ways of spreading light –
to be the candle or the mirror that reflects it.
*Edith Wharton*

# Real Strength

Lord, be gracious to us; we long for You.
Be our strength every morning,
our salvation in time of distress.
- Isaiah 33:2 -

Do you want to be a strong woman? Well, who doesn't want to be able to stand up for herself? Who doesn't hope that she can stand strong for what she believes? What does strength mean to you, though?

Some see rigidness as strength. These people kind of live inside a box that has clearly defined rules. They are often not very accepting of any who do not fit inside their box. Others are more flexible and while that may not seem like strength at first view – it actually is. Women who are more flexible have opportunities to build relationships with people who have a different mindset. The importance of this is that you can't share your faith walk with people you do not have relationships with. Be willing to bend in order to be strong.

The bamboo that bends is stronger
than the oak that resists.
*Japanese Proverb*

# Planning Ahead

The plans of the Lord stand firm forever, the purposes of His heart through all generations.
- Psalm 33:11 -

Planning ahead. Some people are very good at lists, plans and projects. Other people live in the moment and do not think much about the future and what they need to do to prepare for it. Once in a while God gives a direction about something to do to prepare for the future. It's wise to pay attention to that because you don't know what the future holds.

If Noah had ignored God's instruction to build the ark, he and his family would have drowned in the great flood – in fact, mankind would have been wiped out. Pay attention to ideas God puts in your heart, even if they don't make sense at the moment. You have no idea what He has planned and how He wants to use you to make the plan happen!

It wasn't raining when Noah built the ark.
Howard Ruff

# Joyful Play!

Splendor and majesty are before Him;
strength and joy are in His dwelling place.

- 1 Chronicles 16:27 -

Being a grown-up is a big responsibility. We have to support ourselves, do our work, take care of our homes, handle big crises ... it is pretty serious stuff.

Do you sometimes feel that you've gotten so "grown up" that you don't really have fun anymore? Can you remember any of the fun of being a child? Do you wonder why you should? Well, think about it ... when children are having fun, being spontaneous in their play, they are filled with joy.

Joy should be more a part of life, even for grown-ups because God has created a wonderful, beautiful, creative world for us to live in. Every single thing you do does not have to have a serious purpose – loosen up, have some fun and worship with joy as you toss an unexpected snowball!

The aging process has you firmly in its grasp if you never get the urge to throw a snowball.

*Doug Larson*

# Faith with Feet

Because of the Lord's great love we are not
consumed, for His compassions never fail.
They are new every morning;
great is Your faithfulness.
- Lamentations 3:22-23 -

## Dear God,

I'm scared. I need a job and I've answered every ad
I've found, but nothing has happened. I want to work.
Even though I'm older, I still have a lot to offer an
employer. But none of them have been able to see that.
I've been rejected for every interview. Now, I've just
had one more and the job seems perfect for me ... plus
it's the only option I've got right now. So, I sit here
by my phone trying to hope ... trying to have faith
that this will be the one. I said *trying* to hope because
doubting is easier – that way I won't be disappointed
when the answer is "We've gone with someone else."

Please, God, help me to have hope. Help me to have
faith. Help me to remember that You are involved and
You do care about this situation.

Amen.

Hope is putting faith to work when
doubting would be easier.
*Anonymous*

# Give Away a Smile

May the Lord make your love increase
and overflow for each other and for
everyone else, just as ours does for you.
- 1 Thessalonians 3:12 -

Busy city streets packed with people. Proper "city etiquette" is to not make eye contact with anyone as you rush down the street. Ever wonder why? Going into shops, cafes, stores, does the "no eye contact" rule still apply? It often seems to, and that means that the world is full of isolated people rushing through their days, dealing with whatever issues each one has.

When you think about it, a simple smile might help someone get through their day a bit easier. There is a connection that happens when one stranger smiles at another – it says, "You're a person. I see that. I acknowledge that you are sharing this planet with me – we're in this together." It's kind. It's caring. It's one simple first step in sharing God's love with another person. It might make all the difference for that stranger.

Today, give a stranger one of your smiles.
It might be the only sunshine he sees all day.
Quoted in P.S. I Love You,
compiled by H. Jackson Brown, Jr

# Instructional Prayers

He says, "Be still, and know that I am God;
I will be exalted among the nations,
I will be exalted in the earth."

- Psalm 46:10 -

True confession time ... your prayer time consists mostly of ... ? There are several recognized types of prayer: praise, intercession, thanksgiving and telling God exactly what He should do. Which one is your speciality?

When something weighs heavy on your heart, of course you want to pour it out to God and even "suggest" how He should handle it. After all, prayer is communication with God and by definition communication is a two-way conversation. But, how often does your prayer time include quiet listening? After you've given God your suggestions on how to handle a situation, how often do you take time to be still and see if He has something to say to you?

Giving God that quiet time will undoubtedly enhance your relationship with God as you give Him a chance to speak to you. Only by listening can you hear.

The trouble with nearly everybody who prays is that he says "Amen" and runs away before God has a chance to reply.

*Frank Laubach*

# Rookie Status

Do not be anxious about anything,
but in every situation, by prayer and petition,
with thanksgiving, present your requests to God.
- Philippians 4:6 -

If worry counted as a spiritual gift, I would be a spiritual giant! I can't count the hours and energy wasted on worrying about what might happen, what could happen or even what could never happen ... but will certainly happen to me. Sigh.

I am through with worry! As of right now I'm turning over a new leaf. I'm turning in my Master Worrier status in exchange for a Rookie Truster status. I'll accept the rookie status because I know it is going to be a journey to learn to trust God in all aspects of my life.

But, it is what I want to do. Trust the One who loves me more than I can imagine. Trust the all-powerful, omnipotent God. Whew ... wonder what I'm going to do with all my free time now! Do you want to join me in exchanging worry for trust?

If I had my life to live over,
I would perhaps have more actual
troubles but I'd have fewer imaginary ones.
Don Herold

# The Second Greatest Commandment

Let us consider how we may spur one
another on toward love and good deeds.
- Hebrews 10:24 -

Jesus said that the first and greatest commandment is to love God with all your heart, soul, mind and strength and the second is like it, love your neighbor as yourself (Matt. 22:38-39). That sounds pretty simple, doesn't it? Unfortunately it isn't always simple. Living in families, working in community, just being around other people can sometimes get on your last nerve until your temper flares, unkind words are shouted and life is not fun for anyone.

So, how do you obey that second greatest commandment when you have to live around people? Take the focus off yourself and the insistence of always getting your way. Think about others first and pray ... a lot. There are times when you just don't have the necessary love to give to someone who is wearing that last nerve thin, but God does. Ask Him to give you the strength to allow Him to love through you and to keep your heart, temper and touch gentle and kind.

Have a heart that never hardens, and a temper
that never tires, and a touch that never hurts.

*Charles Dickens*

# Effective Prayer

Search me, God, and know my heart;
test me and know my anxious thoughts.
See if there is any offensive way in me,
and lead me in the way everlasting.
- Psalm 139:23-24 -

Have you ever tried to lose weight? How serious were you about this effort? If you made a big show about it in front of others, eating dry salad and plain tuna fish, all the while talking about your diet, but then went home and ate cookies and ice cream in private – well, you weren't too serious.

When it comes to dieting, you can't have it both ways. The same is true with prayer. You may have the ability to speak beautiful, holy sounding prayers with real conviction in your voice, but if you are hiding secret sins, the effectiveness of your prayers is compromised. Pray first for your own cleansing and ask for God's forgiveness – connect with Him on a deeper level – then move forward in prayer.

If the Christian does not allow prayer to drive sin
out of his life, sin will drive prayer out of his life.
Like light and darkness,
the two cannot dwell together.

*M. E. Andross*

# Smile of Love

Love is patient, love is kind. It does not envy,
it does not boast, it is not proud. It does not
dishonor others, it is not self-seeking, it is not
easily angered, it keeps no record of wrongs.
- 1 Corinthians 13:4-5 -

You and a good friend had a serious misunderstanding. Angry words were spoken on both sides and now you haven't seen each other for a while. One day you walk into your favorite coffee shop (in fact, the place where you and your friend used to meet) and lo and behold ... there she is. You see her just as she picks up her latte and turns from the counter. The moment she sees you a frown spreads across her face. Then time seems to freeze as you stare at each other, both wondering what will happen next.

One of you could do something that will change everything – smile. Let a gentle, friendly smile spread across your face and it will confuse that frown on your friend's. Your smile will be an overture of peace. Remember the gentle but firm command from the Father to show love, to be love ... to simply love. Don't hold grudges; value friends and just love.

A smile confuses an approaching frown.

*Anonymous*

# Work in Progress

The Lord is faithful, and He will strengthen you
and protect you from the evil one.
- 2 Thessalonians 3:3 -

You are becoming. That doesn't mean you are a pretty lady (though I'm sure you are). This "becoming" speaks of you as a person and it means you are a work in progress. That progress continues for your entire life. Are you happy with where you are in the progress journey right now? Maybe you look at your life and see failures instead of progress – too much negativity or lack of discipline or self-centeredness.

There are certainly those seasons in life when it feels like you are not making any progress – not going anywhere and you feel dissatisfied and discouraged. But, remember that as long as you're alive, God is still working on you and in you so don't give up. Just thank Him for who you are and how far you've come and keep allowing His work in your heart to make you the woman you will become!

Give thanks for what you are now, and keep
fighting for what you want to be tomorrow.
*Fernanda Miramontes-Landeros*

# Oppressive Darkness

You will be secure, because there is hope;
you will look about you
and take your rest in safety.
- Job 11:18 -

Have you ever been in a place like this: Darkness all around you? Darkness so deep that you can't see your own hand in front of your face. You've been there a while and can see no hint of light at all. You have no idea if anyone is in the room with you.

In fact, you're not sure that anyone even knows where you are. The darkness is oppressive and you have little hope of rescue. Darkness this deep is caused by different things: job loss, illness, broken relationships, habitual sins you can't stop ... sometimes it is the silence of God. Yes, there are times when even the presence of God is hard to sense in that darkness.

But, even in the oppressive darkness and seeming silence of God, faith means believing He is still there and that He does care very much about you. So, hold out our hand, stand up, believe that God is with you. Have faith.

Hope is faith holding out its hand in the dark.

*George Iles*

# A Mom's Advice

The one who has knowledge uses
words with restraint, and whoever
has understanding is even-tempered.
- Proverbs 17:27 -

If you can't say something nice, don't say anything at all. Did your mom ever give you that advice? Very good advice, but, unfortunately, some people have difficulty putting it into practice. Knowing when to keep your opinion and statements to yourself is wisdom at work. Being able to do it is strength and kindness.

Sometimes you can fully enjoy the people around you, even if you do not agree on all things. Conversation can be invigorating, stimulating and challenging. But, some people get very "in your face" with their opinions (which are always right). Those are the times when, to show God's love and kindness to others, you must endure and just be quiet. Arguing seldom changes another person's mind and only serves to damage relationships.

So, heed your mother's advice and know that you are showing love to another by doing so!

Enjoy when you can, and endure when you must.
*Johann Wolfgang von Goethe*

# Prayer Changes Things

I call on You, my God, for You will answer me;
turn Your ear to me and hear my prayer.

- Psalm 17:6 -

God knows best. God knows best. God knows best. You know that's true but when you are in the middle of stress, fear, anxiety and blatant unknowns, it is a difficult fact to hold on to. So, you pray ... and pray and pray and pray for God to do something.

Usually you even tell Him what to do, which kind of negates the whole "God knows best" idea. But, the point is that you do turn to Him and of course, you tell Him what you want, because that is what we people do. Have you noticed, though, that as you are instructing Him, your prayers subtly begin to change? Prayer does not necessarily change God or His plans, but as you spend more time with Him, it does change you and what you desire.

It aligns you more with what God had in mind all along. So, yes, prayer changes things.

Prayer does not change God,
but it changes him who prays.

Søren Kierkegaard

# Spiritual Exercise

Not only so, but we also glory in our sufferings,
because we know that suffering
produces perseverance; perseverance,
character; and character, hope.

- Romans 5:3-4 -

Baking bread from scratch, without the aid of a bread machine, is not as common as it used to be. However, if you've ever done it, or seen it done, you know that kneading the dough is a very physical process. It involves being very rough with the dough in order to make better bread.

To carry through this example, strengthening your spiritual muscle – your heart – will take some stresses and strains. Your automatic response to struggles may be to pray for God to relieve it. That's the response of most people. However, even as you pray for relief, strive to remain faithful and strong in your walk with God and this spiritual exercise will strengthen your faith.

Recognizing that God is always with you in good times and difficult ones will help you see these struggles as part of the process to grow stronger in faith – spiritual exercise.

Is bread the better for kneading? So is the heart.
Knead it then by spiritual exercises;
or God must knead it by afflictions.

Augustus William Hare and Julius Charles Hare

# Uniquely You

"Before I formed you in the womb I knew you,
before you were born I set you apart;
I appointed you as a prophet to the nations."
- Jeremiah 1:5 -

True confession time – does the opinion of others in your world influence you to try to change yourself to please them? Come on, be honest. From a controlling mom to an opinionated mother-in-law to an influential friend, do you find yourself tweaking your opinions, behaviors, activities or even appearance to please these people more?

It's difficult sometimes because some people are very vocal about what they think others should do or be. One good reason not to let this happen is that God made you to be you. You are unique and special and that's a good thing.

If you begin to change things about yourself, even slowly and one thing at a time, pretty soon there isn't much "you" left and the unique person God created has become a cookie cutter version of a lot of other people. Save yourself!

He who trims himself to suit everyone
will soon whittle himself away.

Raymond Hull

# The Last Word

"Therefore, if you are offering your gift at the altar and there remember that your brother or sister has something against you, leave your gift there in front of the altar. First go and be reconciled to them; then come and offer your gift."

- Matthew 5:23-24 -

Did you ever have a disagreement with someone and as the verbal barbs fly back and forth your tempers begin to rise a bit. That keeps the argument going, doesn't it? Things end up being said that neither of you mean but as tempers rise so does the sting of the verbal attack. This can quickly lead to a damaged or even broken relationship that may never be repaired.

So, how can you stop this from happening? When the verbal arrows are being shot back and forth, use one of your turns to apologize. Yep, just take a deep breath and say, "Look, I've said some things I don't really mean. I'm sorry. I value your friendship too much to let it be ruined this way. Will you forgive me?

It is difficult to keep arguing when a sincere apology has been offered. God puts a high value on healthy relationships and friendships so take yours seriously.

An apology is a good way to have the last word.

*Anonymous*

# True Friends

Now these three remain: faith, hope
and love. But the greatest of these is love.
- 1 Corinthians 13:13 -

Women are pretty good at friendships.
Friends are very important to most women. However,
friendships come in layers. Most women have a lot
of acquaintances. Those are people you greet and
with whom you exchange small talk. Most women
have several casual friendships. Those are people with
whom you might chat on specific topics such as work
or favorite books to read.

Most women are blessed to have one or two really
good, close friends. These are the friends with whom
you can share the depths of your soul – good and
bad. These are the friends who truly care how you are
doing and want to share your joys and hold your hand
through the sorrows. These friends are rock solid and
will always be there for you.

True friends are a gift from God, so if you have
one or two, celebrate. If you are one to someone else ...
celebrate!

Friends are those rare people who ask how
you are and then wait for the answer.

# A Sweet Perfume

Follow God's example, therefore, as dearly
loved children and walk in the way of love, just
as Christ loved us and gave Himself up for us
as a fragrant offering and sacrifice to God.
- Ephesians 5:1-2 -

When I'm frustrated and generally crabby the last thing I want to hear is someone's happy talk. I want to enjoy my crabbiness and just wallow in my unhappiness. After all, my bad attitude doesn't hurt anyone except me, right? Not so.

A bad attitude and critical spirit spreads like a bad odor to those who come into contact with me. I pull others down to my level. It's not pretty. However, the opposite is also true. If I can maintain a positive attitude and make a real effort to treat all I meet with love and kindness, that will also spread to others. What a joy to be able to spread the love of God to all I meet.

By allowing God's love to flow through me, I can be like a sweet perfume to others so they will be better off by having been with me.

Spread love everywhere you go. Let no one
ever come to you without leaving happier.
*Mother Teresa*

# Grief and Fear

May our Lord Jesus Christ Himself and God
our Father, who loved us and by His grace
gave us eternal encouragement and good hope,
encourage your hearts and strengthen
you in every good deed and word.

- 2 Thessalonians 2:16-17 -

You've just said goodbye to someone you loved with all your heart. It's been a long journey to get to this final goodbye. You're tired and emotionally spent and now filled with grief. The emotion of grief is consuming and what may surprise you, as it did C. S. Lewis, is that a big part of grief is fear.

As you take the next step into life without your loved one, you feel fear about how you're going to handle life without that special someone. Fear about what life looks like now. Fear of being alone. Fear of being lonely. So, what do you do? Two things come to mind ... first is allow your friends to be there for you. Let them in to your fear and grief. The second and most important is to remember that you are never alone. God is with you. He knows how your grief and pain feel. He cares. Lean on Him and let Him love you. You will get through this.

No one ever told me that grief felt so like fear.
C. S. Lewis

# Cooling Down

The tongue also is a fire, a world of evil among
the parts of the body. It corrupts the whole body,
sets the whole course of one's life on fire,
and is itself set on fire by hell.

- James 3:6 -

My grandmother used to cook with a pressure cooker. It was an interesting piece of kitchenware that uses boiling water to build up pressure inside a sealed pot. The idea is that the food inside cooks faster but my grandmother always had a fear that she hadn't properly closed the cooker and therefore the lid might come blasting off and hurt whoever was nearby. Yeah, when something blasts off, people nearby will get hurt.

The old adage to count to ten before speaking or losing your temper is a great idea. It makes you take a moment (actually ten moments) before you "lose it" and that gives you a chance to cool down. Sometimes you need even more help, so pray and ask God to prolong your patience. Then, even though your patience may be gone, you won't blast in to someone and damage a relationship. Remember to thank God for His help!

Patience is the ability to count
down before you blast off.

*Anonymous*

# A Year-Long Journey

"I will instruct you and teach you in
the way you should go; I will counsel
you with My loving eye on you."

- Psalm 32:8 -

**Birthdays are tough** when that first number
changes, aren't they? At least once you reach a certain
age they are because you sense that the years are flying
by and your time on this planet is, too. How do you
handle the journey?

As you grow older do you find different ways to be
useful and of service to God? Or are you more content
to settle down with a good book and let the hours pass
by? Of course, there is nothing wrong with reading
and relaxing but recognize that this journey called
life will come to an end one day and you don't get to
collect wasted days at the end.

Don't you want to make the most of the time
you have here? Be sensitive to how God leads you to
change your activities and how you will spend your
time as you grow older. Let Him guide you into
new areas. Make the most of every 365-day journey
around the sun!

A birthday is just the first day of another
365-day journey around the sun. Enjoy the trip.

*Anonymous*

# Lovin' the Journey!

The Lord your God is with you, the Mighty Warrior who saves. He will take great delight in you; in His love He will no longer rebuke you, but will rejoice over you with singing.
- Zephaniah 3:17 -

You know the type — a person who always sees the glass as half-empty and cannot celebrate the half-full glass. She is a tiring one to be around because nothing is ever good enough, big enough, rich enough or happy enough. She worries about every problem or even potential problem. The potholes of relationship struggles, minor illnesses, job stresses, money issues and various other things suck the joy right out of her life. This doesn't describe you, does it? Hopefully not.

Life is a journey and there are good times and hard times. There will be joys and sorrows. But the joy of this journey is that you never make it alone ... God is with you every step of the way and not a single thing ever surprises Him. So ... celebrate!

Stop worrying about the potholes in the road and celebrate the journey!

*Barbara Hoffman*

# Big Meal of Small Bites

Those who hope in the Lord will renew their
strength. They will soar on wings like eagles;
they will run and not grow weary,
they will walk and not be faint.
- Isaiah 40:31 -

My friend is about to lose her home. She lost
her job about a year ago and used up her savings when
she had a serious illness with no health insurance.
Now she can't make her mortgage payment so she will
probably lose her home. Life is overwhelming to her
right now and she doesn't even know where to begin
to start the process of salvaging life; packing up her
home, finding a place to live, finding a job, regaining
health ... it's a big job.

But the only way she can do it is a step at a time.
She must come up with a plan and then be willing
to follow the process that will take her to the result
she wants. She is praying about this – a lot. And I'm
praying with her for God's guidance and a real sense
of His presence as she begins this painful journey. I
pray for light and joy at the other end!

You must eat an elephant one bite at a time.
*African Proverb*

# Trail Blazer

"Have I not commanded you?
Be strong and courageous. Do not be afraid;
do not be discouraged, for the Lord your
God will be with you wherever you go."

- Joshua 1:9 -

Right foot. Left foot. Heel to toe. One foot in front of the other. Many people live their lives by following a trail that someone blazed long before them. There is nothing wrong with that. It keeps established companies and ministries going. But if you are bored with walking the same old path, if God has placed a yearning in your heart to do something different or do some established thing in a different way; then you may become a trail blazer.

Be willing to follow God off the beaten path. See where He leads you and be open to what He wants you to do. Blazing a trail can be scary – but filled with enormous rewards that you could never have imagined. Be open to the unknown. You will be enormously blessed!

Do not go where the path may lead, go instead
where there is no path and leave a trail.

*Ralph Waldo Emerson*

# New Pathways

If anyone, then, knows the good they ought
to do and doesn't do it, it is sin for them.

- James 4:17 -

Same old same old same old. Do you sometimes feel as though everyone around you is doing
new and exciting things but you're stuck in the same
old rut? Is part of that your own fault because you're
so cautious that you aren't willing to take a chance
and learn something new?

Life is not static. It is always changing so if you
aren't willing to change with it, you will be left doing
the same old same old same old. Learn a new skill.
Master a new computer program. Take dance lessons.
Volunteer for the refugee ministry at your church.
Try something new. Yes, it will be a process to learn
it, but as you learn from day to day, you will grow and
change.

You may never know where God is leading you if
you aren't willing to explore a new pathway.

Unless you try to do something beyond what
you have already mastered, you will never grow.

*Ronald E. Osborn*

# Real Abundance

Dear friends, let us love one another,
for love comes from God. Everyone who
loves has been born of God and knows God.
- 1 John 4:7 -

The way of our world, especially in America, is to work hard and make lots of money in order to buy lots of things. We want more, more and more. There is even a sense of failure if we do not have the "things" that those around us have.

But what is real abundance? Clear your mind for the moment of all the gadgets, toys and things that are already in your possession or on your wish list. What is left in your life that really matters? This is the abundance you should concentrate on – a strong relationship with your God; opportunities to serve Him and others; family and friends who love you. Abundance is not really "stuff." It is relationships – beginning with God and then moving on down the list. Don't let your focus get stuck on accumulating things that keep you equal with others in the world's eye. Focus on relationships. That's true abundance.

Abundance is not something we acquire.
It is something we tune into.
*Wayne Dyer*

# Light of Love

There is no fear in love. But perfect love drives
out fear, because fear has to do with punishment.
The one who fears is not made perfect in love.

- 1 John 4:18 -

Life is going to have problems. There are no
two ways about it. There are ups, downs, bumps in
the road and flat out failures. How do you handle
the difficulties of life? What gets you through them?
Do you gorge yourself on cookies and candy to make
yourself feel better? Doesn't work, does it? Do you
spend money that you don't have? Never a good idea.
Do you drink a little more wine than normal? Doesn't
help either, does it? Do you depend on your friends to
pick you up? Friends are great, but is there something
even better?

Yes, there is something better than all these things –
the God who loves you. Turn your face into the warm
light of His love, and as today's quote says, the shadows will fall behind you. Life will look more hopeful.

Things will eventually get better and until they do,
God's light will warm you and guide you.

When you face the sun,
the shadows always fall behind you.

Helen Keller

# The Strength of Job

I pray that the eyes of your heart may be enlightened in order that you may know the hope to which He has called you, the riches of His glorious inheritance in His holy people, and His incomparably great power for us who believe. That power is the same as the mighty strength He exerted when He raised Christ from the dead and seated Him at His right hand in the heavenly realms.

- Ephesians 1:18-20 -

Women have a reputation for being very relational beings. We expressively care for others. We sometimes take their problems and pains into our own hearts along with our personal problems. Suffering is overwhelming and when you care for the people who are hurting, it can be oppressive. But, do you know the story of Job? His suffering was deep and ongoing and yet he never turned against the God he loved and whom he believed loved him.

When your suffering quotient is overwhelming, remember that God is walking with you. Draw strength, even from the pain itself and determine to move forward, stand strong and SURVIVE whatever you are facing. God is your strength. He is your endurance. He is your provider. You are never alone.

We shall draw from the heart of suffering itself the means of inspiration and survival.

Sir Winston Churchill

## Other Books in the
## *GodMoments* series

*GodMoments for Moms*

*GodMoments for Men*

*GodMoments for You*